PRACT
CONSCIOUSNESS

PRACTICAL CONSCIOUSNESS

Mastering the Art of Living

Isaac David Shamaya, Ph.D.
Carolyn Shamaya, M.A.

SAMUEL WEISER, INC.

York Beach, Maine

First published in 1994 by
Samuel Weiser, Inc.
P. O. Box 612
York Beach, ME 03910–0612

Library of Congress Cataloging-in-Publication Data

Shamaya, Isaac David
    Practical consciousness : mastering the art of living /
  by Isaac David Shamaya and Carolyn Shamaya.
        p.   cm.
    Includes index.
    1. Conduct of life.   I. Shamaya, Carolyn.
  II. Title.
BF637.C5S53   1994
158'.1—dc20   94–20550
                                                        CIP

ISBN 0–87728–810–0
MG

Cover art copyright © 1994 Ananda Kurt Pilz. Used by
permission of the Walter Holl Agency, Germany.

Typeset in 11 point Baskerville

Printed in the United States of America

99 98 97 96 95 94
10 9 8 7 6 5 4 3 2 1

The paper used in this publication meets the minimum
requirements of the American National Standard for
Permanence of Paper for Printed Library Materials
Z39.48–1984.

To Melinda Nixon—
a great teacher and beloved friend

Table of Contents

A Note to the Reader ix
Introduction xi

Part I: Ground of Being

Insight 1: Going with the Flow. 3
Insight 2: Don't Ask Why 5
Insight 3: Befriend Each Moment 7
Insight 4: Want What Happens 9
Insight 5: Personal Preferences Secondary 13
Insight 6: Living Beyond Desires. 15
Insight 7: Re-evaluate Values 17
Insight 8: Possessions in Perspective 19
Insight 9: Cultivate Self-Love 21
Insight 10: Enjoy Being Ordinary. 23
Insight 11: Honor the Body 25

Part II: Emotional Life

Insight 12: Compassion for All 29
Insight 13: Value Every Emotion. 31
Insight 14: Show True Feelings 33
Insight 15: Free of Guilt 35
Insight 16: Emotional Grounding. 37
Insight 17: Stress-Free Living 39

Part III: Relationships

Insight 18:   Being Is Loving........................43
Insight 19:   Intimacy with Life.....................45
Insight 20:   Sharing, Yes! Comparing, No!..........47
Insight 21:   Communicate Feelings Honestly........49
Insight 22:   Internal Well-Being 51
Insight 23:   Victims No More!......................53
Insight 24:   Say No to Blame! 55
Insight 25:   No Need to Get Even 57
Insight 26:   Live and Let Live 59
Insight 27:   Free of Arrogance 61

Part IV: Vision

Insight 28:   Life Is a Mystery 65
Insight 29:   A Sense of Wonder....................67
Insight 30:   Free of Judging.......................69
Insight 31:   Be Here Now..........................73
Insight 32:   Trust Real Feelings....................75
Insight 33:   Owning Experience 77
Insight 34:   Value Not Knowing 79
Insight 35:   Responsibility for Behavior 81
Insight 36:   Be Sincere, Not Serious!................83
Insight 37:   Free of Beliefs 85
Insight 38:   Free of Opinions 87
Insight 39:   Remember, All Is Well.................89
Insight 40:   Free to Be.............................91
Insight 41:   Live in Delightful Uncertainty 93

Conclusion...95
Index...99
About the Authors.................................104

A Note to the Reader

Anyone who has studied psychology is familiar with a course titled "Abnormal Psychology." Has anyone ever heard of a course offered in "Normal Psychology"? There are reams and reams of material written about mental illness and millions of dollars spent on research. Even a visit to the self-help and psychology sections of the local bookstore reveals that most titles focus on what is wrong with us as human beings. We are alternately described as addicts, co-dependents, or neurotics. We are women who love too much and men who can't open up. We are suffering from depression, lacking in self-esteem, and starving for love. We are the victims of abuse, incest, and neglect. According to many of the books, most if not all of us are leading dysfunctional, unhealthy lives.

Practical Consciousness is a book that dares to be different. It paints a simple, yet vivid picture of what life is like once we are living healthy lives instead of dysfunctional ones. What is our state of mind when we're no longer dysfunctional? What is our emotional state? What are our relationships like? The answers to these questions are addressed in the following pages.

Having been trained as mental health professionals, we have counseled hundreds of individuals and their families over the course of our careers. We've read hundreds of books and spent hundreds of dollars to be trained by experts in our respective fields. But, the most important preparation of all for writing this book has come from a sincere commitment to grow into conscious, mentally healthy people. Difficult life circumstances including the death of a child, the death of a parent, divorce, the loss of jobs, have all provided opportunities for emotional and spiritual growth.

In this book, we share what we've learned—both personally and professionally—about the state of mental health. We recommend that the following material not be read in a hurry, devoured page after page. Each of the 41 insights is like a hearty meal that deserves some time to be adequately digested.

We understand the state of mental health to be our natural state, our very birthright. Therefore, we don't need to "do" anything in order to achieve it; it is simply who we are. We have written this book so those reading may come to realize their true nature in a deeper way than ever before.

Introduction

Practical Consciousness presents delightful and insightful anecdotes and stories relating to mental health and an overall sense of well-being. It addresses how we can live in this ever-changing world with some semblance of grace, goodness, and self-respect. In 41 short essays called "Insights," you learn what it takes to experience the world as a place of wonder and beauty rather than a place of conflict and suffering. Unlike many self-help books that take themselves so seriously, this book is playful and irreverent as it shines a warm, supportive, resourceful light on the human encounter with life.

We think that the essence of ancient mystical teaching can be understood in a plain, earthy, common-sense kind of way, guaranteed to tickle your funny bone. It shows you how to replace fear and suffering with a sense of spiritual, emotional, and physical well-being. When Kermit the Frog of "Sesame Street" sang "It's Not Easy Being Green," most people related to him. We related because every one of us could sing a similar refrain—"It's not easy being human." Life, like the weather, is subject to changes beyond our personal control. Some days are sunny and our circumstances harmonious; other days are cloudy and the circumstances are depressing. Sometimes it storms and if we venture out, we get drenched and the winds of change blow us about like fallen leaves or angels. Given life's unpredictability, and a world where the force of gravity dictates that what goes up must come down, is there a place to be inside ourselves where it is always safe and joyful to be who we are? *Practical Consciousness* poses this question and answers it 41 times with a resounding, "Yes!"

Mental health involves much more than just being able to "function and cope" in the world. It involves consciously participating in your own life and a commitment to growing in self-awareness and self-acceptance. This commitment turns life into an adventure in self-discovery and self-actualization whereby it becomes possible to realize the unique, creative potential within and live a truly fulfilling life.

Practical Consciousness is a perfect complement to working a 12-step program, practicing meditation, participating in group therapy, going to counselling, doing yoga, or just having an interest in personal growth. It can be read over and over again because it will reveal new insights previously unrecognized. In addition to nourishing and strengthening your innermost being, it's a book you'll have great fun reading.

PRACTICAL
CONSCIOUSNESS

PART I

GROUND OF BEING

INSIGHT 1
GOING WITH THE FLOW

L ife is quite an amazing trip! Just when it appears we're headed where we want to be going, we run smack into a roadblock that forces us to take a different route. Suddenly, we find ourselves in unfamiliar territory. Then we discover how resourceful and creative we really are. Such unexpected changes, when things start going differently than we hoped they would, give us the opportunity to see where we're still stuck in old patterns of belief and behaviors. As someone once said, it's easy to be loving and creative in heavenly circumstances. The question is, can we be loving and creative when we're going through hell?

Most of us were taught that to have expectations is a perfectly normal part of life. Yet, when we expect things to go a certain way, or believe we need them to go that way, we can be blind to the reality of what is actually happening. For example, it is not uncommon for a person to apply for a particular job with the expectation or hope of getting it, only to be offered a different job instead. And even though the job offered could turn out to be the perfect stepping stone, the person rejects the whole situation out of hand because the original expectation wasn't met.

Very often, there is a strong emotional investment that goes along with an expectation; and when something doesn't happen the way we expect it to happen, we get upset, sometimes very upset, and can spend hours, days—or even the rest of our lives—stewing in the soup of emotional resentment and self-pity.

Mentally healthy people understand that life doesn't always go according to preconceived or hoped for plans. Thus, they live relatively free of expectations. Since they know they are not capable of controlling the flow of life, they don't resist the natural unfolding of events. Rather, they embody a capacity to respond to unexpected changes gracefully, without suffering the prolonged fear and frustration that can result from rigid expectations. The courage to stay open to what life brings and the willingness to find unforeseen opportunities in the midst of life's unexpected twists and turns constitute a mentally healthy outlook.

When he was spokesperson for American Express Karl Malden, of TV fame, offered some excellent advice every time he spoke those immortal words "Don't leave home without it!" Forget about the American Express card; think about it as a willingness to go with the flow of life. If there were a club for mentally healthy people to join, it's motto might very well be, "We take it as it comes."

✦ INSIGHT 2
DON'T ASK WHY

Kurt Vonnegut, the famous novelist, was speaking to a group of aspiring young writers about their craft. In his talk he encouraged them to only write about what happens in the story. Basically, he said it was ridiculous to write about why things have happened because we do not and cannot know. And he is absolutely right, because everything that happens in the universe is interconnected with everything else. Thus, even the most brilliant human mind is not capable of fully understanding exactly why events happen as they do.

In fact, any such endeavor is basically a way of deluding ourselves into thinking we really understand what the heck is going on in this mad, mad world when we can't — and don't need to either. The need to figure out why personal events happen as they do is essentially a futile, and therefore, stressful pursuit. Even though our minds are very practiced at dreaming up explanations for anything and everything, such explanations are always limited (partial truths) and limiting. For example, if we believe that our ongoing unhappiness comes from having been raised in a dysfunctional family, we automatically limit our potential to stop suffering since the past is never going to change.

Healthy people place a premium on the value of direct experience rather than intellectual analyses and beliefs. They realize that it is only through direct experience that they can know anything of reality; therefore, they pay attention to it rather than focusing on what the thinking mind has to say by way of explanation. The fact of the matter is that even if it were possible to mentally grasp why personal things happen as they do, such information would have absolutely nothing to do with living fully and functioning effectively in the world.

Woody Allen once said, "Nothing worth knowing can be understood with the mind." And Albert Einstein once said, "All knowledge of reality begins in experience, and ends in it." Who would've ever thought that Woody and Albert shared a similar point of view, relatively speaking, of course!

✦ INSIGHT 3
BEFRIEND
EACH MOMENT

Whatever is happening at any given moment happens to be all that's happening! Given that, we each have a choice. We can either struggle against what is happening, or we can embrace it. It's really that simple. It's easy to tell when someone has chosen to live life as a struggle. Typically, such a person engages in activities like whining, complaining, finger-pointing, and criticizing. These activities are basically unhealthy, for they do little other than perpetuate misery, suffering, and stress in daily life. That's because what we resist, tends to persist.

Mentally healthy people have no interest in living life as a struggle. For them, life is a perpetual embrace—they are lovers who embrace their present experience as if it were their beloved. This is so even when their experience is an unpleasant one. At such times in particular, much like when a friend is not feeling well, they see that life is calling upon their capacity to feel compassion. Their point of view here reflects the wisdom of Malcolm Muggeridge who said in his memoirs, "Contrary to what might be expected, I look back on experiences that at the time seemed especially desolating and painful with particular satisfaction. Indeed, everything I have learned, everything that has truly enhanced and enlightened my existence has been through affliction and not through happiness."*

Regardless of what is happening, mentally healthy people see each and every moment as an opportunity to experience themselves anew and respond to each situation accordingly. Then they are able to let go into the experience of the next moment. Nothing is judged. Nothing is rejected, or, conversely, held on to. If there is a moment of insight, for example, they embrace the insight experience fully. If they lose a loved one, they embrace the experience of loss fully. Every moment is welcomed as an affirmation of the aliveness within them.

Lived in this way, life is reminiscent of a song most of us learned as children: "Row, row, row your boat gently down the stream. Merrily, merrily, merrily, merrily, life is but a dream." And so it is!

---

*Malcolm Muggeridge, *Chronicles of Wasted Time: An Autobiography* (Washington, DC: Regnery Gateway, 1989).

8

INSIGHT 4
WANT WHAT HAPPENS

I n the Great House of Life, we can only leave the room of Inner Conflict, down in a dark and dingy basement, through the door that says "Total Acceptance." Mentally healthy people walk through that door and into the light nearly every moment of every day. Their reference point could best be described as one of affectionate detachment. They have discovered how secure life is when they don't fight against it, or judge that something is wrong with the way things have happened. They remember that all is right—even that which seems wrong.

There is an old story that comes to mind here. It's about a little song sparrow named Henry. Henry was a rather remarkable young bird, bright and cheery, a born leader from the time he popped his head through the shell. We could say that all his life he'd listened to the beat of a different woodpecker.

One autumn, as winter was fast approaching, and the other song sparrows were preparing to fly south, Henry announced to the whole sparrow community that he wasn't going with them that year. He said he had decided it was time for a sparrow to break with that particular tradition. It was time, he said, to explore new realms, so he was going to stay in the north for the winter.

Henry's pronouncement caused horror and dismay among the other sparrows. His friends and relatives pleaded with him to reconsider. First, they tried to make him feel stupid. "Boy, Henry, you sure are a jerk." When that failed, they tried to make him feel guilty. "How can you do this to us when we love you so much?" But his mind was made up, and in late October, Henry said good-bye to all his friends and relatives as they left for warmer climes.

The next few weeks were wonderful. Henry absorbed everything that was happening around him. For the first time—and that was the first time in sparrow history, mind you—he saw the autumn leaves fall from their branches. He delighted in their windblown movements as they fluttered to the ground. Sometimes he would fly under them and keep them afloat for a little while before they fell to the earth. He was having a grand time.

But, as the weeks passed, Henry began to be bothered by the increasing cold. The first snowfall, which came in late November, was very painful for him. His feathers became encased in a thin layer of ice, making it very difficult to move his wings. When the second snowstorm almost killed him, he began to think seriously about flying south to be with the other sparrows. Yes, he decided, if he was going to survive, he had to get where it was warmer. So, on a gray, January morning, he took off in a southerly direction. Before he had flown more than five miles, ice began to form on his wings. Unable to support the added weight of the ice, he fell to the ground in a crumpled little heap.

As his frozen mind cleared, he opened his eyes and saw he had landed in the middle of a barnyard. Just then, an enormous animal he recognized as a cow appeared. He saw the cow walking toward him, but he was too stiff and cold to flutter from the path of the great hooves. Just as the cow was directly above him, it stopped and—to his utter astonishment and horror—emptied its bowels. As the cow dung poured down on top of him, Henry thought, "Oh no, now I'm surely going to die." But it didn't take more than a few seconds for Henry to realize that the cow dung was warm . . . wonderfully warm! In fact, it felt so good he stuck his head out of the pile and began to sing.

Well, as fate would have it, a cat in the barnyard heard Henry's chirping and came over to investigate. Upon seeing the young sparrow on the ground, the cat pulled Henry out of the cow dung and ate him.

Henry did not die in vain, however, because his story has three important morals. First, people who seem to shit on you are not necessarily your enemies. Second, people who pull you out of shit are not necessarily your friends. And third, if you're warm and happy in shit, keep your mouth shut!

 INSIGHT 5
PERSONAL
PREFERENCES
SECONDARY

(M) ost of us make choices in the world on the basis of what we believe is pleasurable. We are constantly concerned with seeking pleasure (comfort) and avoiding pain (discomfort). Unfortunately, all too often life becomes a frantic search for ways to control inner and outer circumstances; a search for a pleasureful high that will never end. Mentally healthy people, on the other hand, act on a different basis. They tune into themselves at a deeper level than mere selfish pleasure. It is a level where they sense what feels "right" to them in their hearts whether the resulting experience is pleasurable or not. This way of being in the world allows for living with a sense of integrity and commitment and a deep feeling of well-being and joy.

Two of the personal qualities that are of great value in living with integrity and commitment are flexibility and adaptability. Mentally healthy people do not have to have their own way. In situations where their preference doesn't affect anyone other than themselves, like choosing their ice cream cone flavor, they go for exactly what they want. But in situations involving other people, they are likely to fit in and cooperate with others, rather than insist on having things their way. Such behavior on their part does not involve any sense of self-sacrifice at all. On the contrary, by acting on the basis of what they feel is right, rather than on what might feel good, they derive the great satisfaction that only comes from living with integrity.

There is a wonderful story that illustrates the principle under discussion here. It's about a young unmarried woman who lived in a small fishing village in China. One day, she met and fell in love with a young sailor who was visiting her village in the course of his travels. He, too, fell in love and promised her he would one day return to marry her after he had found his fortune.

As fate would have it, she became pregnant and gave birth to a daughter nine months later. When the child was born, her parents felt disgraced and angrily demanded to know who the father was. Not wanting to reveal the identity of her true love, she said the father was Long Chen, a monk who lived in the hills above the village. Outraged, her parents took the child to Long Chen's hut and pounded on his door. When he opened it, they handed him the baby saying, "This child is yours; you must care for it." "Is that so?" said Long Chen, taking the child and waving good-bye to the parents as they left in a huff.

One year later, the sailor returned to the village to marry his beloved. At once the two lovers went to Long Chen to plead for the return of their child. "We must have our daughter," they said. "Is that so?" said Long Chen, handing the child to them and waving good-bye as they joyfully walked toward the village.

 **INSIGHT 6**
LIVING
BEYOND DESIRES

(T) here are many differing ways to view the role of desires in our lives. For example, William Blake spoke of desire as being "holy." On the other hand, Oscar Wilde, in his inimitable fashion once said that in this world he found only two tragedies—not getting what you want, and getting it.*

Regardless of our particular point of view on desires, one thing is abundantly clear; if we let our sense of self-satisfaction or self-esteem be dependent upon having our desires fulfilled, then we're in trouble! Whether we like it or not, sometimes things work out the way we want, and sometimes they don't. This is simply the way it is—and it's that way for everyone, regardless of social standing or material wealth.

Mentally healthy people have a lasting sense of self-satisfaction and self-esteem. Paradoxically, it is this positive regard for themselves that allows them to be unselfish and not self-centered in their relationships. Such a positive sense of self exists beyond whether or not their personal desires get fulfilled. It has to do with an abiding appreciation of themselves just the way they are, regardless of the frustration or fulfillment of their desires.

---

*Oscar Wilde, *Lady Windermere's Fan*, act 3.

Mentally healthy people appreciate who they are uncon-ditionally; thus, their inner state is not dependent upon outer circumstances. They have an overriding and ongo-ing sense of fullness within, which comes from knowing that they are whole and complete. Because they don't feel lack within, they are able to live beyond their desires. For them, it's not such a big deal whether or not they get what they want. Their approach to life is very balanced. It brings to mind an old joke, "Do you know why angels fly?" The answer is "Because they take themselves lightly!" And so do mentally healthy people.

INSIGHT 7
RE-EVALUATE VALUES

In general, it's our view that life is too important to take seriously. But here's a question worthy of some moderately serious consideration: must we, as individuals, automatically value what others value and do as others do? So many of us seem to believe in and do exactly what we've been told by our parents, teachers, religious leaders, etc.—the so-called "proper authorities." Many of us apparently have not found it relevant to question the values imposed on us in early life. To live in this way is to live without any real sense of our personal uniqueness and individuality. Essentially ruled by blind faith in the values of others, we go through life doing what we *should* or *ought* to do, feeling what we *should* or *ought* to feel, and thinking what we *should* or *ought* to think. Instead of being the vibrant, creative people we can be, we end up living like automatons leading lives of quiet desperation.

Through the media, as well as through personal contact with other individuals, we are constantly exposed to people with value systems different from our own. As a result, we always have opportunities to review old values and find deeper personal truths within. One of the sure signs of mental health is the willingness to let go of old values and understandings in favor of new ones that allow for relating to the world with greater honesty, integrity, awareness and love.

17

The ultimate value of any particular understanding is its ability to plant seeds of new understandings. Therefore, to see our current point of view or value system as the complete and final word on anything is a misunderstanding.

Mentally healthy people have taken a good, honest, critical look at the values they were taught to believe as children. In the process, they have chosen to keep for themselves only those values that have "the ring of truth" to them, discarding the rest. Thus, they are not compelled to act according to "should" or "ought to" but are free to respond creatively on the basis of their true feelings. Hearing "the ring of truth" is not merely a metaphor but an actual inner experience. When resonating deeply with a particular point of view, it's as if a subtle tone or vibration goes off in the body. The awareness of this tone is how mentally healthy people know what is right and true for them as individuals. In fact, they have realized that such an awareness is the only reliable source of information they can count on to guide them in daily living.

Shakespeare wrote "To thine own self be true."* These words beautifully express the *modus operandi* of mentally healthy people. Ultimately, trust placed anywhere other than in our own true feelings is misplaced trust. Furthermore, if we do not trust ourselves, we cannot know whether or not to trust anyone else. Is it any wonder, then, that there's so much distrust in the world?

*William Shakespeare, *Hamlet,* act 1, sc. 3, line 79.

INSIGHT 8
POSSESSIONS
IN PERSPECTIVE

Henry David Thoreau spoke of wealth not in proportion to what an individual has, but in proportion to what he or she can do without. This lovely bit of wisdom stands in stark contrast to the way most of us have been taught to think about wealth. We live in a culture that espouses the belief that more is better, that life is about having things, and success is to be measured in terms of material monetary gain. Mentally healthy people do not adhere to this belief; for they know that real and lasting satisfaction is a kind of self-satisfaction. It does not and cannot come from getting and having things. It must come simply from *being*. They have discovered that the secret of life is in honest and free self-expression, and that is their sole (soul) concern. They have realized that it is only by expressing themselves honestly and freely in response to life that they can gain the satisfaction they yearn for. This satisfaction is found in the ordinary things they say and do throughout each day. In the long run, such a focus is far more valuable than that of accumulating more and more material possessions. In fact, that which we are unwilling to give away, we do not possess, but are possessed by.

In being fully themselves, conscious people contribute their unique brand of aliveness to every scene in the play of their lives without worrying about what's in a given situation for them. Thus, they have realized quite naturally the wisdom inherent in the saying, "Caring is sharing and living is giving."

Self-actualization is the focus of mentally healthy people for they have realized this: it is by and through the actual expression of themselves, moment by moment, day by day, that they come to find that which everyone is longing for—fulfillment.

There is, of course, the school of thought that proposes as an ultimate focus finding the best pizza in town and eating it as often as possible. Let us not entirely discredit this point of view. After all, there are times when eating great pizza can be nourishment for the soul as well as the stomach!

✳ INSIGHT 9
CULTIVATE SELF-LOVE

Two of the most important qualities of mentally healthy people are self-respect and self-appreciation. These qualities allow them to respond to others with respect and appreciation. Any time we act in ways that are disrespectful or unappreciative of another person, we can be sure that deep down we believe there is something wrong with who we are.

The notion that there is something wrong with us is usually implanted in our minds early in life. It most often comes from parents or other relatives who, consciously or unconsciously, believe there is something wrong with themselves. They then projected their negative beliefs about themselves onto us, sometimes in a very innocent fashion. As impressionable and dependent young beings we assumed their views, and out flew our self-esteem; that is, until we realize that those adults were sadly mistaken—not only about us, but about themselves as well.

Mentally healthy people have a strong, clear awareness of their human goodness. This awareness, which accompanies the feeling of self-respect and appreciation, allows them to express themselves freely without ever feeling guilty. They are absolutely comfortable with themselves and are not preoccupied, therefore, with a need to improve or change. Rather, they intuitively understand that by being open to what life brings, they will surely receive whatever they need to develop and grow naturally into fuller, more complete expressions of themselves as a loving presence in the world.

The actor Henry Winkler said, "A human being's first responsibility is to shake hands with himself."* That is how mentally healthy people start every day. They meet themselves, greet themselves, and go about the business of being themselves. Although this doesn't magically make life a piece of cake, it does allow us to enjoy our daily bread.

---

*Quoted by Jim Gallagher in *Detroit Free Press,* reprinted in Reader's Digest's "Quotable Quotes," 1991.

✦ INSIGHT 10
ENJOY BEING ORDINARY

So much of the pressure we experience in daily life comes from an exaggerated sense of self-importance or specialness. Television advertising would have us believe that we are better and more deserving than others, that we are special, not in the sense of being unique, but in the sense of being superior. When we believe that we are more important than we really are, we tend to take things very personally—particularly when things don't go the way we want them to go. For example, have you ever had the experience of standing in line to get into a movie only to find that just as you get to the box office the tickets are sold out? When something like this happens, people who believe they are special tend to react by feeling abused and may even become hostile. In contrast, insightful people are likely to see the humor in such a circumstance, even if they feel disappointed about not getting into the movie. What allows mentally healthy people to respond in this way is their sense of ordinariness. Of course, they realize that they are unique individuals, but they don't think of themselves as being any better or more worthy than anyone else.

Accompanying this sense of being ordinary is a deep feeling of humility and an identification with the trials and tribulations of all humanity. Mentally healthy people recognize that we're all in this predicament called life

23

together. Their point of view, which honors the worth of all human beings, lends itself to living with ease instead of dis-ease, and cooperation rather than competition. In terms of William Shakespeare's metaphor, "All the world's a stage,"* mentally healthy people see themselves simply as members of the cast on the great stage called planet Earth. They know they are no more or less important than any of the other players; and, by themselves, they take neither the credit nor the blame for the way any given scene turns out. Nonetheless, they play their part as fully as they can, simply giving outstanding performances of who they really are.

Sometimes the truth can best be expressed in the form of a paradox: It's only when we stop thinking of ourselves as special that we become special. Furthermore, remember the nursery rhyme about Humpty Dumpty. Yes, it can be dangerous to put ourselves above others!

---

*William Shakespeare, *As You Like It*, act 2, sc. 7, line 139.

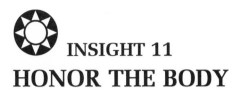

INSIGHT 11
HONOR THE BODY

here is a definite link between mental health and
physical well-being. The ancient Greeks knew this
and formulated the well-worn phrase, "Sound
body, sound mind." Or is it the other way around? Regardless of which comes first, it's wise to satisfy our physical needs by eating healthfully, exercising daily, and resting plenty.

Mentally healthy people are imbued with a great deal
of self-respect. An important aspect of that respect is taking care of the body's needs, not in an obsessive or worri-
some way, but very easily and naturally. The billions and
billions of cells that make up the healthy physical body
are all working together in concert—each with an amazing awareness of its unique part in the functioning of the
totality. It is possible to experience our body as if the cells
are "alive with the sound of music," to borrow a phrase
from the popular Broadway show. Mentally healthy people truly appreciate their bodies' inner musical produc-
tion, and see fit to provide a healthy dose of loving care to
the body in order to maintain the overall condition of
their physical instruments.

In some ways, the antithesis of mental health is
demonstrated by those individuals whose lives revolve
around the recurring belief that something is physically
wrong with them. Hardly a week passes that they don't go

to visit one physician or another. Their strange love affair with illness is like a debilitating addiction, and they suffer untold misery again and again.

As more and more people grow into mental health, there will be less and less dependence on medical treatment since people will maintain excellent physical health well into their later years. Recent medical research on aging indicates that there does not appear to be much of an aging process at all in healthy tissues. It seems that only in unhealthy, diseased tissues is there a deterioration process that occurs over time. Thus, mentally and physically healthy people can look forward to growing old without the chronic debilitation often endured by the elderly.

Of all the people we've known in our lives, there is one in particular who truly manifested the many insights into mental health. At age 94, while out taking a brisk walk one morning, our friend was struck by a car and died a week later. In the autopsy report the doctor wrote the following: "Based on the condition of his internal organs, he could have easily lived another fifty years." Pretty amazing, huh? Yes, there certainly is a connection between mental health and physical well-being.

PART II

EMOTIONAL LIFE

INSIGHT 12
COMPASSION FOR ALL

In Webster's dictionary, compassion is defined as "a feeling of tenderness directed toward the personal discomfort in oneself or another." From our (the authors') perspective, this is a very good definition; but it doesn't go quite far enough. Not only is compassion a tender feeling, it often has a behavioral component as well. Compassion is actually nature's way of responding to pain, and mentally healthy people, being deeply in touch with their nature, often behave in compassionate ways. The following true story from nature is a beautiful illustration of compassion in action.

A house cat had caught and badly injured a bird in the back yard of a midwestern family. Before the cat could kill the bird, the cat was chased away by its owner, who then tried to offer help to the injured bird. But every time the well-intentioned woman got near the bird, it went into a frenzy, flapping its wings violently. Finally, the woman decided it was best to leave the fallen bird in peace, and she returned to her kitchen. A short time later, while looking out the window, she noticed another bird flying close to the injured one. As she looked on, this other bird, with male markings, flew to a nearby tree and alit next to a nest in one of the tree's branches. At that point, the woman realized the nest was filled with baby birds. Then she saw

29

the whole picture, realizing that the injured bird was the babies' mother, and the male was the father.

Over the next few weeks, the woman watched in fascination as the father bird worked himself to exhaustion flying back and forth from the nest to feed not only the baby birds, but his fallen mate as well. Somehow, he managed to keep all of them alive until the time came for the babies to leave the nest. The father then took on another job—coaxing the baby birds to try out their wings. Their first flight took them to lower branches in the tree near where their mother lay on the ground. At this point, the father bird began to harass the mother bird, encouraging her to fly just as he had coaxed the little ones. At first she would only flap her wings pitifully, and then give up in seeming despair. But the father bird kept after her to fly, and on the third day, she actually lifted herself off the ground. Several days later, she flew to the branches of the tree and was reunited with her family.

The father bird's behavior in this true story illustrates the real meaning of compassion. It shows us what's possible in this world as more and more of us awaken to our essential human nature, and in the process, experience what it is to be mentally healthy.

✸ INSIGHT 13
VALUE EVERY EMOTION

Everyone knows that some feelings are comfortable to experience while others are uncomfortable. Many people have learned to block out of their awareness feelings they don't like. This process, called denial, often happens automatically—that is, without any conscious awareness or intention on the part of the person in denial. The only problem with denial is that it doesn't work. We cannot get rid of a part of ourselves—in this case, an uncomfortable feeling—and expect that part of us to heal. This would be like cutting off a finger in order to heal a hangnail—it just doesn't make sense.

Chances are we grew up with parents who had a terrible misunderstanding about how feelings work. They believed that when they stopped us from crying or having a tantrum, that took care of our difficulties. They thought that by interrupting the expression of our feelings, the feelings were eliminated. But that's not how feelings actually work. When their expression is interrupted, the feelings in question don't disappear. Rather, they go into a state of denial. When feelings are denied, the energy associated with those feelings cannot be released. That energy gets stuck in the body where it is held in the cells and disturbs the natural, healthy functioning of our physical apparatus. Eventually, this held energy causes the body to break down, and one form of illness or another shows up.

31

In addition, if we are unwilling or unable to acknowledge and express a particular feeling, we are doomed to suffer experiences that call forth that feeling over and over again. This is why, even at a personal level, history seems to repeat itself.

Mentally healthy people are readily willing to experience all of their feelings—the uncomfortable as well as the comfortable ones. They realize that their feeling/emotional nature is actually a valuable guidance and protection system, offering them information that is not only trustworthy, but essential in daily decision-making. Aware of what they feel, they spontaneously know the optimum response to make in each situation. They recognize that there is never anything wrong with what they feel. In fact, feelings are not mentally classified as positive or negative. Neither are they considered morally good or bad. They are simply valued as the current manifestation of aliveness in any given moment. Each and every feeling that arises is thus welcomed into conscious awareness; for to do otherwise, is to indulge in self-deception. Mentally healthy people have no interest in playing the self-deception game, knowing that its inevitable outcome is always an increase in personal suffering. Their game is real aliveness, played with emotional honesty on a field of mutual respect and appreciation for all feelings—theirs as well as those of others.

The great American social historian and mythologist, Joseph Campbell, spoke to this point. He disagreed with people who believe that what human beings are seeking is the meaning of life. He felt that what we're really seeking is the moment by moment experience of being alive. The experience of being alive is exactly what mentally healthy people value above all else. How do we know we're alive? We feel it! Without feelings, we're as good as dead.

❖ INSIGHT 14
SHOW TRUE FEELINGS

Of all the experiences human beings can have in this life, the experience of shame is one of the most debilitating. Shame stems from a deeply held belief that it is not okay to be who we are and feel what we feel. Clearly, it is inconsistent with the state of mental health.

In a widely shown television commercial for a camera, a world-renowned tennis star says, "Image is everything." But the fact of the matter is that when we believe we have to uphold a certain image of ourselves, we are likely to feel conflict whenever we have an experience that does not foster that image. When we believe there is something unacceptable (unloving, unworthy, etc.) in us, we learn to live a life of pretense—a life in which we cannot reveal our true feelings to the world. So whenever we experience unacceptable feelings or emotions, we pretend to feel other than what is really felt. In effect, we become ashamed of ourselves, and life becomes an ever more complicated affair in which we cannot relax and simply let the truth be revealed.

Mentally healthy people, on the other hand, are not ashamed to be who they are. Nor are they ashamed to express how they really feel. They do not judge or doubt their feelings; they trust and respond to them. Instead of a shame-based reality, they sense that whatever they feel in any given circumstance is exactly right for them. As a result, they are not ashamed and are indeed free to be open and honest. This does not mean they feel compelled to act out their feelings; on the contrary, it is the acceptance of feelings that enables us to choose how and when to express those feelings.

Furthermore, mentally healthy people understand that self-confidence is related to the ability to *confide* in others—to openly and honestly express their innermost feelings. The people who honor and respect their openness and honesty are recognized as true friends; and mentally healthy people tend to value their friends as much as, if not more than, anything in the world.

For mentally healthy people, life is not a complicated affair, but a rather simple unfolding of events which continuously offers the opportunity for honest self-expression. This attitude is beautifully summed up in the words of an ancient Chinese sage who said, "Since everything in life is but an experience, perfect in being what it is and having nothing to do with good or bad, acceptance or rejection, one may as well burst out in laughter."

Tee-hee!

INSIGHT 15
FREE OF GUILT

(A)lthough we often hear people say "I feel guilty," guilt is not actually a feeling—it's a mental judgment. It's as if our intellect accuses us of wrongdoing, puts us on trial, usurps the role of judge and jury, and reaches a verdict against who we are as individuals. Then it's as if we stand convicted of some terrible crime—and our suffering begins. The irony is that this whole process takes place only in our imagination.

When we judge ourselves guilty, we often experience an underlying feeling of fear. The fear stems from a subtle anticipation of the punishment we are due for our imagined crime—just as in the judicial system a judgment of guilt is followed by sentencing. This entire guilt scenario is a self-fulfilling prophecy—if we believe in the intellect's judgment of guilt, we will always face life circumstances that appear to be punishing. Even though we may not like the punishing circumstances, and may believe life is treating us unfairly, deep down we believe we deserve to be punished, because in our mind's eye we stand convicted.

For starters, mentally healthy people do not live by their intellect. They pay very little attention to the mind's judgments, and thus do not suffer from guilt. They realize that the intellectual process of "judging and jurying" is a gross misuse of the mind. They understand that in the

35

real world things that have already happened could not have happened any differently due to all the contingencies leading up to each situation. More to the point, mentally healthy people experience themselves as innocent— not as saints, but in the way all of nature is innocent. Even when natural events appear destructive and unkind, there is no malicious motive at work. Neither is there a malicious motive at work in human nature most of the time; and they see that this is so in themselves and others as well.

In *The Mists of Avalon,* Merlin makes the following statement which relates to this point: "We will do what we always have done—what we must, what the Gods order. We will do the best we can."* Isn't that the truth for all of us?

---

*Marion Zimmer Bradley, *The Mists of Avalon,* New York: Knopf, 1982.

 **INSIGHT 16**

EMOTIONAL GROUNDING

There is an old joke that relates to this symptom: People who are neurotic build castles in the sky; people who are psychotic live in them; and psychiatrists collect the rent! It is a fact that many of us invest lots of time and energy fantasizing about what life could be, should be, or would be if only _____ (you fill in the blank). We often do this instead of responding to life as it really is.

Most of us grew up listening to fairy tales and children's stories that ended with those six tragic words, "And they lived happily ever after." These words, implanted in our innocent, young minds, have had tragic consequences because they do not accurately describe reality. We (the authors) wonder how much suffering has resulted from those six, innocent-sounding words! Hearing them over and over again in our childhood is perhaps the basis of our neurotic tendency to build castles in the sky. Perhaps we'd have been better off if we'd heard stories that ended with the words, "And they lived on as best they could ever after," revealing the truth that life can sometimes be quite difficult, and not every situation has a happy ending. Then, instead of dreaming about the future, we might have our feet on the ground and know where we stand in the present. Such a grounded awareness is an important part of mental health.

Mentally healthy people have seen through the illusory promise of life in everlasting happiness. They realize that life has its ups and downs, that we live in a world where the force of gravity is operational; thus, what goes up must come down. They don't try to hold on to the good times or escape the bad. They know that everything changes, so they do not get too high or too low as a result of changing circumstances. Instead of measuring their life against some idealized fantasy, such as living happily ever after, and despairing when things aren't going well, or exulting when they are, they maintain a well-balanced, even-keeled emotional state throughout.

Honestly, have you ever know anyone who is living happily ever after here on Earth? The fact of the matter is, as expressed by Merlin the Magician in *The Mists of Avalon*, "We are none of us embarked on this course for our own happiness. Whatever we may do to try to shape our destiny, the end is with the Gods."* In other words, conscious people open to life as it is in each moment rather than controling it to invent their own happiness. Paradoxically, such people discover in the process that life is really much more enjoyable that way!

---

*Marion Zimmer Bradley, *The Mists of Avalon*.

INSIGHT 17
STRESS-FREE LIVING

here is a commonly held, albeit mistaken, notion that stress is caused by external circumstances. Actually we experience stress whenever we close off to what's happening in life. In essence, it arises when there is a psychological (and sometimes physical) resistance to whatever is going on at the moment. The calling card of mentally healthy people is a quality that's best described as "relaxed aliveness." Instead of getting uptight and withdrawing from their experience in difficult moments, they open to life regardless of what is happening. They figuratively and literally breathe easy in all situations.

Speaking of breathing, there is a direct relationship between how we breathe and how much aliveness we embody. The deeper and fuller our respiration is, the more we feel; and the more we feel, the more in touch with life we are. Mentally healthy people breathe diaphragmatically (deeply), and the rising and subsiding of their thoracic cavity with each breath can be observed. It is always possible to tell whether we are stressed out or not by watching our breathing. When the breath is held, and appears very shallow, it's a good bet that we are feeling under stress—even if we're not aware of it.

The cells of our bodies are constantly hungering for oxygen in order to function at their optimum level. Thus it is our natural state to breathe deeply and freely. Just look at the way animals and newborn babies breathe. The lack of respiration (chronic shallow breathing) can be both the cause and the effect of stress. Mentally healthy people are not stressed out about the external circumstances of life. They have chosen to experience every moment with the greatest degree of aliveness and awareness possible. To that end, their respiration is deep and full throughout each day. There is no great effort needed to breathe this way, for once we stop resisting life and surrender to our true nature, the body's natural wisdom takes over and full respiration happens by itself.

In one of the American Indian languages, the term for "making love" literally means "to breathe together." This is a beautiful metaphor for the truth that if we all did more breathing and less worrying, the world might very well be a more loving place.

PART III

RELATIONSHIPS

✵ INSIGHT 18
BEING IS LOVING

T he plight of many people is best summed up by the song lyric, "Looking for love in all the wrong places." For mental health, any place outside ourselves is the wrong place to seek love. Insightful people understand love as the natural outcome of a nonjudgmental awareness of themselves and others. They find that love is at the very core of their being, as if it's the heart of all living matter. They recognize love as the very presence of life itself—here from the beginning of time until the end of time. All we need to do is keep recognizing it as ourselves.

When we begin to look inward for the love we've been seeking outside ourselves, we are guaranteed to find it sooner or later. And until we look inward, the love we seek will just keep slipping away. When we believe love must come from outside, we'll repeatedly find that we love someone one day, but not the next; or that someone loves us one day but not the next. It just keeps "slip-sliding away."

Another song lyric that sheds light on the real nature of love is "Love is a many splendored thing." This is, indeed, an insightful phrase; for splendor means "a great brightness." Love is a great brightness, capable of lighting up our days like the golden rays of the sun. The feelings we call affection, appreciation, and compassion are three

43

of love's brightest rays, and qualities that mentally healthy people embody in generous amounts.

We might say that the fundamental relationship in life is that between oneself and one's own heart. All other, outer relationships exist simply as reflections of the state of that inner relationship. Thus, if we hate ourselves, our relationships with others will likely be filled with hate; and if we embody a nonjudgmental appreciation of ourselves; our outer relationships will be filled with love.

Mentally healthy people, having realized such an appreciation of themselves, are not concerned about receiving or giving love, for they are no longer seekers of love but finders. And what have they found? Simply that love is the fabric and also the stitching of this coat of many colors we call the universe. If you aren't aware of wearing it, a coat just your size is hanging there on the rack, waiting for you to put it on whenever you are ready. It will be there forever until you are.

✸ INSIGHT 19
INTIMACY WITH LIFE

T here is a big difference between merely being alive and truly living with aliveness. A person in a coma could be said to be alive, but such a person could hardly be said to demonstrate much aliveness. Over the years, we have discovered a direct relationship between the extent of our aliveness and the degree to which we feel intimately connected with life itself. When we feel apart from whatever is going on around us, instead of a part of what's going on, we invariably develop a sense of alienation and isolation—two major factors in clinical depression, the psychiatric term for living without aliveness.

Intimacy, the healthy alternative to alienation and isolation, is fundamental in the relationship we develop with ourselves. Someone once said that intimacy means "into me I see." This definition is the essence of what intimacy is all about. When we are nonjudgmentally aware of our actual experience from moment to moment, not only do we live with a sense of intimacy, we know what it is to be truly at home with ourselves. This reality is at the very core of mental health. Wherever they may be—whether with someone or alone—mentally healthy people are intimately in touch with themselves, with the actual experience of being alive at each moment. Their awareness is constantly filled with what it feels like to be present in the world. When with another person, they focus on the experience of being with that person rather than concerning themselves with what they think about or perceive in the other person or what the other person might be thinking about or perceiving in them.

This way of being in the world is the exact opposite of what has become known as co-dependency. In essence, people who are co-dependent focus almost exclusively on mental thoughts and perceptions of what's going on around them—particularly regarding what they imagine other people are experiencing. These people are not aware of their own inner experience or feeling most of the time and therefore never have a sense of personal empowerment.

The fact is that it's not possible to have a lasting, intimate relationship with another person until you first know an ongoing intimacy with yourself. Is it any wonder then that people who are co-dependent remain in a perpetual state of hunger for a satisfying relationship with another person? There's a revealing joke about co-dependency that asks, "What do co-dependents experience when drowning, as they're about to go under for the third time?" The answer is "They see someone's else's life flash before their eyes." Without an ongoing awareness of what it feels like to be you, you really have no life of your own!

✦ INSIGHT 20
SHARING, YES!
COMPARING, NO!

(T)he so-called rational mind is always dividing the world up into separate pieces and then making comparisons between one piece and another. It's become almost second nature for us to believe that such divisions are real and such comparisons important. When we relate to the world in a strictly conceptual/intellectual way, in effect we are enslaved by our thoughts. Consequently, we tend to get lost in our imagination and lose touch with our basic human nature. This is generally unhealthy because it is a denial of a deep-seated, natural inclination to respond to life on the basis of true feelings.

When we first came into the world as newborn babies, we had no thinking mind. There were no words, no concepts, no judgments, no beliefs; there was only an awareness of what it felt like to be alive, and a natural response (sharing) to whatever feeling was present. For example, if we were uncomfortable, we cried; if we felt pleasure, we cooed.

All the thoughts and beliefs we learned as we were growing up have served to interfere with this natural incli-nation to share ourselves spontaneously on the basis of our true feelings. Mentally healthy people are those who have gotten back to their basic human nature and recov-ered this inclination. They demonstrate an increasing willingness to let themselves be deeply touched by the people and circumstances of their lives. Above all, mentally healthy people accept themselves for being who they are, and this allows them to accept others for being who they are. The fact that they embody certain relative strengths and weaknesses in comparison to others makes absolutely no difference to them—for differences are not equated with inferiority or superiority. Instead of judging differences, mentally healthy people celebrate life's diversity and appreciate the unique qualities each person embodies. Furthermore, the result of comparing ourselves to others is that we end up feeling disconnected from them, as well as from ourselves.

By simply sharing instead of comparing themselves, they realize the wisdom in the old proverb: A happiness shared is a happiness doubled; whereas a sadness shared is a sadness halved.

✵ INSIGHT 21
COMMUNICATE
FEELINGS HONESTLY

Most relationships run into problems because of a lack of honest communication. When such communication is absent, misunderstanding is heaped upon misunderstanding and the aliveness in the relationship is eventually buried six feet under. The more important a particular relationship is to us, the more important it is to communicate honestly in that relationship. In general, honest communication consists of two parts; telling the other person exactly how we feel without blaming or holding that person responsible for our feelings; and saying what we want from the other person, while not presuming he or she is obligated to give it to us.

Insightful people are experts at honest communication. They are not afraid to reveal their true feelings and desires to others and are willing to take their chances on being rejected for their honesty. They also appreciate it when others are willing to be honest as well. When confronted with another's honesty, they do not get defensive or critical. Neither do they withdraw emotionally from the relationship when the going gets tough.

Sometimes problems arise when we communicate what we want from another person and then don't get it. This is not a problem for mentally healthy people, however, because they are willing to accept any situation as it is. This includes taking responsibility for any uncomfortable feelings (disappointment, anger, etc.) they experience, without blaming or resenting the other person.

An Old English proverb states, "Many things are lost for want of asking." Of course, there is no possibility of honest communication when one or both people in a relationship are unaware of how they are feeling or what they want from each other in a given situation. It is the steady focus on, and acceptance of, their feeling/emotional nature that, more than anything else, characterizes mentally healthy people. They are deeply in touch with their experience of being alive; thus, they are able to express what is really true for them whenever they deem it important to do so.

By letting others know where they stand, they make it possible for others to respond with a clear view of the situation at hand. This is actually a wonderful gift to give to others. Usurping a phrase from a well-known soap commercial, "It takes the worry out of being close."

INSIGHT 22
INTERNAL WELL-BEING

We live in a world where there is a prevalence of addictions. Whether it's alcohol, drugs, sex, gambling, greed, power—you name it—there are many people who seem to need something outside themselves in order to feel alive and good about life.

Webster's dictionary defines an addict as one who has "surrendered to something habitually or obsessively." This definition immediately brings to mind the biblical commandment: "Thou shalt have no other gods before Me" (Exodus 20:3).* In effect, addicts bow down to the object of their addiction as if it were their god. Thus, addicts believe they cannot get through daily life without the object of their addiction—alcoholics without a drink, drug addicts without dope, sex addicts without getting laid, gamblers without a bet, workaholics without overtime, and so on.

Basically, people develop addictions because they do not feel at home with themselves. Deep down they feel alienated (like an alien), even in their own home or community. So they turn to one addiction or another in order to escape what has become a very painful reality.

In contrast, mentally healthy people feel absolutely

---

*From the King James version of the Bible.

51

at home with themselves. They experience a kind of self-appreciation, which is independent of what is happening with anyone or anything outside themselves. For example, the mentally healthy do not need to have other people change or behave in a certain way in order to feel fine about who they are as people. They see that individuals who depend on others in this way often end up in very difficult and painful situations.

When we feel truly at home with ourselves, we can echo the immortal words of that great spiritual teacher, Popeye the Sailorman, "I am what I am and that's all that I am." With these words we experience an ongoing sense of real personal power—regardless of whether we eat our spinach or not!

✴ INSIGHT 23
VICTIMS NO MORE!

There is an old Chinese proverb, "You can't prevent the birds of sadness from flying over your head, but you can prevent them from nesting in your hair." When we see ourselves as victims, in effect, we choose to let the birds of sadness nest in our hair. In order to understand this, it is necessary to understand the distinction between pain and suffering. Pain is simply a feeling of discomfort, which can be either physical or emotional in nature. When we accept the experience of pain without feeling sorry for ourselves—without making a negative mental judgment against the pain—we do not suffer our pain. It is only when we resist the experience of pain by concluding it is bad or wrong to feel it that suffering comes into the picture. If we believe we are victims, we set ourselves up to suffer prolonged pain and, in effect, let the birds of sadness nest in our hair.

Mentally healthy people have no use for suffering in their lives. They accept the experience of pain when it is present and find that it quite naturally flies away. They have discovered that the very nature of experience is constant flow and change.

Mentally healthy people see that, at a core level, they are responsible for everything they experience in life. Therefore, they never perceive themselves as victims, regardless of their circumstances. In this way, they are able to maintain a strong sense of personal power and self-esteem, even in uncomfortable, unwanted circumstances.

Supporting other people who believe they are victims will never help them be free from their victim mentality and consequent suffering. Mentally healthy people understand this and do not verbally agree with others who perceive themselves in that way—even if it might mean losing a particular relationship.

Only by rejecting a victim mentality as a means of relating to the world can we know ourselves as the powerful individuals we really are. After all, if we human beings are truly made in the likeness and image of God, like it says in the Bible, how could we not be powerful?

✦ INSIGHT 24
SAY NO TO BLAME!

When we blame someone for doing or saying something that has made us uncomfortable, in effect we're accusing that person of being responsible for our own inner feeling state. In essence, we're saying to that person, "You made me feel this way." That's like saying "The devil made me do it!" Typically, such a reaction is accompanied by a moral judgment against the person who supposedly caused us to feel the way we do. We take on the role of judge and jury, not only handing down a verdict of "guilty as charged," but doing whatever we can to punish the perceived offender as well.

Clearly, it is not healthy to engage in such behavior, Take a moment to reflect on how you feel when you place blame on someone in this way. It's likely you will find that you don't feel very good inside, because a blaming state of mind tends to be accompanied by a sick inner feeling.

Mentally healthy people are not concerned with finger pointing, fault finding, or blaming others for their own emotional state. They have realized that such endeavors are not only a waste of time and energy, but also perpetuate a feeling of internal dis-ease. In situations where another person might engage in blaming, mentally healthy people take a much more practical tack. They concentrate their energy on releasing their uncomfortable feelings, and make the best out of whatever the present circumstances happen to be. This may mean removing themselves from the circumstances, if that is what feels right for them to do. They don't sulk and don't make themselves heartsick over unpleasant circumstances. They understand that in difficult interpersonal situations the other person has usually done the only thing possible in terms of what he or she believes is right and proper; so it makes no sense to the mentally healthy to blame or attack anyone.

One of the outstanding characteristics of mentally healthy people is that they don't get upset about being upset. There's a moral here somewhere. Perhaps we could promote an anti-blame program. It's motto could be "Just say no to blame!"

INSIGHT 25
NO NEED TO GET EVEN

T here is an important distinction between anger, which is simply an inner feeling, and hostility, which is anger coupled with an accusatory attitude toward the perceived cause of the anger. When we believe we've been wronged by someone, we tend to see that person as our enemy. Then our anger becomes frozen in the form of hostility. Interestingly enough, such a reaction often extends beyond that original person to others who happen to be like him or her. In our culture, hostility is often expressed in the form of verbal sarcasm. The word sarcasm literally means "to bite the flesh of another." Lately, hostility seems to be erupting more often in overt violence as one person, one race, or even one nation attacks another in the name of righting a past wrong. This happens in spite of the fact that most of us have been taught since we were small children that two wrongs don't make a right.

Mentally healthy people do not keep a mental or emotional scorecard of what has happened in the past. They have no interest in seeing others as enemies, even those who have hurt them in some way. Thus, they have no need to hold a grudge against anyone and revenge never enters their minds. They are able to experience anger like the sky experiences a storm—dark clouds gather, there is thunder and lightning, rain falls, and the storm simply blows over. There is no blaming or accusing anyone of anything. Their sole focus in such circumstances is to release the energy of the anger—let it blow over—as soon as possible—for they understand that whenever anyone holds on to ill feelings toward another, they simply make themselves ill.

Recent medical research backs this up with indications that when people figuratively close their hearts to another, it can literally cause a constriction in the flow of blood through the heart. Maybe that's why so much heart disease is around in our present social structure?

If all this is so, as more and more of us become mentally healthy, we can expect to see heart disease become less of a threat in our world. Of course the medical profession would lose billions of dollars spent on procedures like heart by-pass surgery. But maybe it's time for all of us to stop by-passing our hearts!

 **INSIGHT 26**
LIVE AND LET LIVE

T here are many ways one person can try to control the actions of another. Some of the more common are threats ("If you don't do what I say, I'm leaving!"), coercion ("Just one more time . . . please, for old time's sake"), arguments ("You don't know what you're talking about!"), bribes ("If you stay in school, I'll buy you a car for your graduation"), and guilt ("How could you do this to me!"). The main effects of these actions are stress and suffering—usually for both the controller and the controllee.

In reality, we do not and cannot control the actions or responses of other people. People always do what they choose to do, even if they believe they have no choice. This is a point well worth emphasizing: no one does anything against their will regardless of what they may think.

Mentally healthy people know they are responsible for their own actions. This allows them to live free of neurotic entanglements caused by attempts to control others. Instead of trying to control, they prefer to extend to others the freedom they feel within themselves. It's as if they say to others, "What I want is for you to do what you feel is right and best for you." Imagine how you would feel if someone important in your life genuinely and consistently expressed those words to you. Such a message is the foundation upon which all healthy relationships are built.

In a way, mentally healthy people are freedom fighters. In every situation, their words and actions support honest self-expression and mutual respect. Thus, when another person reveals differing values and/or feelings about things, this is not perceived as a signal for conflict and defensiveness. There is no need to control other people by pressuring them to change or defend their point of view. Respecting others' views makes for healthy relationships characterized by individual freedom of expression.

There's an old familiar expression, "Live and let live." That's pretty much how mentally healthy people function in relationships.

INSIGHT 27
FREE OF ARROGANCE

Many of us have encountered people who seem all too anxious to tell us what's wrong with us or somebody else. These people apparently believe they have all the right answers. Not only that, they feel compelled to give their opinions and advice, whether such feedback has been asked for or not. In fact, the need to impress our point of view on others usually stems from deep-seated, and often unacknowledged, feelings of insecurity. Such feelings stand as roadblocks on the way to mental health.

Regardless of the particular philosophy or teaching we might espouse, the message we actually communicate comes through the way we live. Whatever we've learned about life is most powerfully communicated to others simply through our manner of conduct in the matters of daily living. What we practice speaks much louder than what we preach.

There is an important distinction to be made between the intelligence quotient (IQ), which is a measure of the intellect only, and wisdom, which resides in the heart or feeling nature. It is possible to have a high IQ without having much wisdom. Mentally healthy people, regardless of how intellectually gifted they may be, embody a large measure of wisdom evident in several different ways. For one thing, mentally healthy people do not look at others in terms of what's wrong with them or what needs fixing in them. They understand that no one person is really in a position to know what's good, right, or best for anyone else. They see that people who presume to know what's best for someone else can be dangerous. They also understand that, in many instances, the greatest help that can be offered to another person is trusting that person to resolve his or her own problems.

Mentally healthy people don't have big egos that need to be massaged by having others dependent on them for advice or direction. Thus, they don't offer help unless it has been asked for, and sometimes not even then, except for guiding others to find answers within themselves.

As a general rule, it's healthy to respect the rights of others—even their right to make a mess of their lives if they so choose. Someone once joked that people who offer help when it hasn't been asked for often discover that "no good deed goes unpunished!" There's definitely some truth in that statement.

PART IV

VISION

INSIGHT 28
LIFE IS A MYSTERY

A lyric from a song in the Broadway show *South Pacific* is, "Who can explain it, who can tell you why? Fools give you reasons, wise men never try." So many of us have an almost compulsive need to try and make sense out of whatever is happening in life. We are forever focusing on mental explanations of events because such explanations provide us with the illusion that we are capable of controlling the world around us. Well, anyone who has taken an honest look at life knows that much of it makes absolutely no sense at all: the death of a child, for example, or the destruction of an earthquake, or winning a ten-million dollar lottery, for that matter.

When we devote ourselves to the pursuit of reasons to theoretically explain what happens in our personal lives, we essentially end up living in a world of our imagination and not in the real world. In understanding reality at any given moment all that can be said is that it's our entire personal history that has led to the particular circumstances that are present at the moment.

Mentally healthy people intuitively know and accept this. They are not particularly interested in rationalizing the circumstances of life and do not spend a lot of time dreaming up and detailing reasons that supposedly explain what has happened. All they know is that every event occurs at precisely the moment it must occur as the inevitable consequence of everything that has preceded it. Beyond that, they simply stand in awe of the whole, gigantic spectacle of life. They appreciate the unfathomable mystery of being here on Earth and have discovered that the more they surrender to this mystical awareness, the richer and fuller their experience of life is.

As more and more people become mentally healthy, there will be more and more human beings who embrace life as a mystery. So our cities, now populated by yuppies (young urban professionals), will be filled with yummies (young urban mystics). Maybe then we'll be able to address our cities' problems in way that make sense.

INSIGHT 29
A SENSE OF WONDER

(M) ost of us have heard the following sayings many times: "God works in mysterious way," and "Truth is stranger than fiction." These old clichés illustrate something that is important for our discussion of mental health. They point to an understanding of life as a wonderful (full-of-wonder), mind-boggling succession of events. This is actually the sense we embodied when we were little children at play. Just like all healthy children, we simply delighted in the wonder of life. We were not concerned with such things as cause and effect, or the meaning of life, or anything else. All we were doing was playing, giving our attention fully to each new moment, fascinated by the mysterious unfolding of events. We were truly innocent in the sense of being without ulterior motives or preconceived plans. Our minds were not calculating and we were not manipulative in the sense of trying to control a distant future. The present was far too interesting to be concerned about what lay ahead, or behind, for that matter.

In many ways, the state of mental health is a return to this childlike—not childish—awareness. Living with this awareness fosters a certain wisdom about how to live as a human being. This wisdom does not come from having all the answers, but from having no questions—no mental concerns or doubts about the past or future. In effect, mentally healthy people have traded their clever-ness for wonderment. In the process they gain something far more valuable than mere conceptual (mental) under-standing. They gain an awareness we might call "inner-standing"—intuitive, wordless knowing that allows for truly creative self-expression. Purely mental understand-ing is like iron pyrite—fool's gold. It looks impressive, but has little real value. Besides, we tend to get old in a hurry when we lose our marvels!

✦ INSIGHT 30
FREE OF JUDGING

Most of us have been taught that it's perfectly normal to make judgments about how our lives are going. Not only that, but we think that we're clever enough to determine when a given situation is going the way it *should* or *shouldn't* go. Mentally healthy people, on the other hand, see no point in wasting time and energy determining where the events of life belong on a balance sheet of blessings and misfortunes. They understand that in the real world things are seldom what they seem, and rarely do they have enough information to judge what is happening in and around them.

There is a wonderful story about a poor old woodcutter who lived in Europe during the Middle Ages. He and his teen-age son resided in a one-room hut on the outskirts of a small village. Every day the two arose at daybreak and went into the forest to chop trees for firewood. In the late afternoon, they loaded their wagoncart with the wood and took it into the village where they sold it for a few coins.

There was one rather remarkable thing about the old man's circumstances. He happened to own a truly magnificent horse, which pulled his wagon to and from the village. This beast was so outstanding that word of its awesome strength and beauty had spread throughout the land.

One day, a prince came to the village seeking the fabled animal. When the old woodcutter arrived leading the horse, the prince was so impressed that he tried to buy the steed for a great sum of money. But the old man politely responded that he had no interest in selling his beloved animal. Thanking the prince for his generous offer, the old man left the village to return home.

The townspeople were quick to judge the old man a fool for not selling the horse, since the money offered by the prince was enough for him and his son to live in comfort for the remainder of their lives.

Several weeks after the prince's visit, the old man and his son awoke to find the horse gone. Later that day they had to pull the wagon full of firewood into the village on their own shoulders. When the townspeople saw this and inquired as to the horse's whereabouts, they chided the woodcutter saying, "See old man? We were right. You were a fool not to take the prince's money, for now this misfortune has occurred and you have neither horse nor money." The old man answered them saying, "I don't know if this is a misfortune. I only know that the horse has vanished." The townspeople rejoined, "Of course it's a misfortune. You must be an imbecile not to see this." The old man just shrugged his shoulders, and when his wood was sold, he returned to his little hut with his son.

Days passed. Then one morning as the sun came up, the old man looked outside and was astonished by what he saw. Not only had his beloved horse returned, but it had brought ten magnificent wild mares with it. Later that day when the townspeople heard the news, they ran to the woodcutter exclaiming, "Old man, you were right after all. It wasn't a misfortune that your horse disappeared, it was a blessing! For now you have all these horses which you can sell for a good price." The old man responded, "I don't know if it is a blessing to have the other horses. I only know that my horse has returned and I am glad to have him with me again." "Of course it's a blessing," said the townspeople. "How can you be so ignorant?" Again, the old man just turned away and left the townspeople to their judgments.

One week after the reappearance of the horse, the old man's son was attempting to ride one of the wild mares when it reared and threw the boy. He was badly injured. The townspeople ran to the hut when they heard the news. "Old man," they said, "you were right again. It wasn't a blessing that your horse brought the wild horses to you, it was a misfortune. Because now your only son will be crippled for life and unable to help you with your work." And the old man responded, "I don't know if it's a misfortune. I only know my son has been injured. What will come of it, who can say?" But the townspeople continued to insist it was a terrible misfortune.

Several months later, the country in which they all lived went to war with a bordering country. The army came to the village and rounded up all the young men to fight in the battle; all, that is, except one. They left the old man's son because he was hardly able to walk and was not fit to be a soldier. When this happened; the townspeople came to the old man with tears in their eyes. In their grief they said to him, "Old man, you were right again. It wasn't a misfortune that your son got hurt. It was a blessing, because at least you will have him with you while most of our sons will be killed in the war and we'll never see them again." With great compassion in his voice, the old man responded, "Dear people, will you never learn? We human beings can never know enough to judge anything as a blessing or a misfortune. Only God knows enough to do that."

✦ INSIGHT 31
BE HERE NOW

Although we tend not to see it as worrying, most of our thinking about the future or the past is just that—a form of worry. It's amazing how many people spend the majority of their time worrying about life instead of living it. Such mental preoccupation is not only unhealthy, it often makes life seem like a fruitless search for a time of quiet relaxation.

Whenever we are lost in thought, we cannot participate wholeheartedly in what's actually going on around us. Take the act of listening, for example; if we are paying attention to what we're thinking while someone else is talking, we are not really available to receive the communication that is, or more accurately, is not taking place.

Mentally healthy people are essentially free of worry. They live in and for each present moment, without mental concern over what is yet to come or what has already transpired. They simply take care of present business and trust that the future will be taken care of in due time—when it becomes the present. From their point of view, the future is recognized as fiction, and the past, a dream. Since what is real is always the present moment, mentally healthy people could be called realists, as their awareness abides in what has been called "the eternal now." As a result, they do not experience any pressure or stress due to the passing of time, enabling them to stay quite relaxed throughout each day.

Leo Tolstoy said that the two most powerful warriors are patience and time. Insightful people definitely stand on the side of patience. They embody the understanding expressed in these immortal words: "God often comes at the last moment, but She never comes late!"

INSIGHT 32
TRUST REAL FEELINGS

Consider what happens in nature when a plant is cut off from its roots. Can that plant continue to thrive or even survive? The answer is, of course not. Well, in human beings, feelings function like the roots of a plant. Only through the direct experience of our feeling/emotional nature can we become rooted in the ground of our being and receive the nourishment and support we need to prosper and grow.

When we are unaware of what we feel in relation to a particular situation, it's as if our roots have been severed; and we are not so much alive at that moment as we are dying. Many people actually exist this way, day in and day out, unaware of their true feelings and merely re-acting (acting as they have in the past) automatically to most situations without any awareness of the creative process at work. Mentally healthy people, on the other hand, understand the importance of self-awareness and make a practice of paying attention to their feeling/emotional nature at all times. This is not really that difficult. All it takes is a little discipline, and before long, it becomes a very natural thing to do. As a result, they have a deeply rooted sense of what is right for them in any given situation, and use the information received through this channel as a wordless guidance system for determining their responses to the ever-changing contingencies of the real world. They trust this source of information implicitly, and thus, always act on the basis of their inner, heartfelt knowing of what is right for them. This is what is required in order to live with integrity.

Mentally healthy people recognize that every person has a unique prescription for successful living within— much as a seed has within it the blueprint for growth into its mature form. They see that every individual has the capacity to meet and resolve all their difficulties, if only they tap their roots and look to their deepest feeling nature for direction. They must seek solutions not in what they *think* about things, or in what others think about them, but in how they themselves really *feel* deep down. As it turns out, these solutions rarely match the preconceived ideas they have about what it would take to dissolve their problems away.

It is by trusting themselves wholeheartedly that mentally healthy people get to live without the twin torments of insecurity and self-doubt. Won't it be wonderful when all of humanity is rid of those two insufferable pests!

✦ INSIGHT 33
OWNING EXPERIENCE

T here is a great misunderstanding, one that is commonly accepted, about the way feelings work. Most of us have been taught to view our feelings as reactions to what is happening around us. A particular circumstance arises, as if by chance, and we react to that circumstance with certain feelings, either positive or negative. But, just as the image of the outer world on our retinas is upside down, so is this view of our inner feelings upside down—that is, it is actually the unique constellation of feelings we embody that calls forth the specific circumstances in our lives, and not the circumstances that determine our feelings.

In one important way, feelings are like the weather. It is their nature to "move out" (the literal meaning of the word "emotion") rather than stay put. Toward that end, feelings function by magnetizing the particular circumstances needed to call them forth in our consciousness so that they can be moved out. This process can only complete itself if we are willing to experience and express our feelings, allowing them to release.

Mentally healthy people intuitively understand the creative nature of feelings and, therefore, accept responsibility for their inner state at all times. Regardless of whether they feel pleasure or pain, joy or sorrow, they simply accept whatever feeling is present and thereby allow it to seek its own release. They see that there are no accidents in the universe, and no mistakes either. Albert Einstein acknowledged this fact when he said that God does not play dice with the universe.

It could be said that mentally healthy people are masters in the art of living; that is, they exhibit a certain degree of mastery in their daily lives. According to Webster's dictionary, mastery is defined as "dominion," which is defined as "absolute ownership." In other words, someone who has mastered the art of living is one who takes absolute ownership—responsibility—for everything that happens and everything that is experienced in life. This is the real basis of personal empowerment—the awareness that we are no less than the magnificent creative process itself in human form. And, we don't need to join the Army to "be all that we can be."

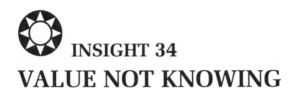

INSIGHT 34
VALUE NOT KNOWING

Some people think they know an awful lot about life. At least they give that impression by the way they expound on everything from politics to religion. For example, how often have we heard someone state a mere personal opinion as if it were the gospel truth? It's hard to understand such arrogance in light of the way such people tend to live their lives.

As a general rule, it's only when we begin to recognize our basic ignorance about what makes the world go round that the door to mental health opens wide. There is an old saying that speaks to this matter of acknowledging our own ignorance: "If we believe we know something about reality, then we really know nothing about it. However, if we know we know nothing about it, then we really know something!"

Every person who becomes mentally healthy must reach the point of knowing that he or she doesn't know. From then on, life is lived with more of an awareness akin to the innocent curiosity and openness of a child. Such openness is actually what allows the wisdom of the universe to be revealed to and through them.

An important part of that wisdom is a deeply felt sense of humility, which has its roots in an appreciation of this awesome adventure called life. Such humility is one of the cornerstones of mental health. In fact, it is a common characteristic in the demeanor of all the truly great men and women throughout history.

Peter Ustinov, the famous actor, made a very interesting observation that relates to this matter of not knowing. He pointed out that courage is often accompanied by a lack of mental understanding (i.e., ignorance) while cowardice, in many cases, is founded on the basis of good information. It takes a lot of courage to consider the possibility that our old, familiar points of view are not the gospel truth. Mental health is inherently born of the willingness to live with some confusion and uncertainty—with the understanding that one does not know. Thus, courage is always one of the essential characteristics of insightful people. The word, itself, comes from the Latin word *cor*, or the French word *coeur* which both mean "heart." So, in order to be mentally healthy, as the old song says, "You gotta have heart. Miles and miles and miles of heart."

INSIGHT 35
RESPONSIBILITY FOR BEHAVIOR

A great deal of the suffering in our lives comes from a commonly held, yet mistaken belief that there are times when we do what we do, not because we want to, but because we have to, or we're supposed to, or we're obligated to, or because we should. Whenever we think "I'm doing what I don't want to be doing" we set ourselves up to experience an inner conflict and all the stress that goes with it. Frequently, this scenario is accompanied by feelings of resentment, frustration, and worst of all, helplessness.

Mentally healthy people are free of inner conflict about their actions in the world. Their understanding is that they are never doing anything against their will. They see that whatever they do is by their own consent and choosing. Thus, no task feels like a burden, and they never feel like a victim of circumstances. For example, if they have a job to do that is repetitive and uninteresting, they accept that it is still something they want to be doing; that is, they are consenting (choosing) to do it. They know they have a choice—they can always walk away from the situation if they so choose.

Some would argue that in certain circumstances we can't walk away because, for example, we have to earn money for food, or provide for our spouse or children, and so on. However, mentally healthy people know they are ultimately responsible for themselves, and their choices in life simply reflect what is really most important to them.

By seeing themselves and their actions in this way, mentally healthy people do not experience the feelings of impotence and self-sacrifice, which often lead others to feel sorry for themselves. Self-pity is never a healthy response. In fact, it is probably the single most important factor in those who suffer from depression.

When we take responsibility for our actions, we are able to live with a real sense of personal power that transcends the pleasant or unpleasant nature of our circumstances. In this sense, responsibility is not a cross to bear but the opportunity of a lifetime. It is the opportunity to realize ourselves as the captains of our ships, the tenders of our gardens, the governors of our states, the leaders of our bands.

✦ INSIGHT 36
BE SINCERE, NOT SERIOUS!

Many people seem to take life very seriously. This is a mistake that can create terrible problems. When we take life seriously, we tend to perceive ourselves in a distorted way. It's as if we're too close to what's happening in our lives, and we lose all perspective and objectivity about ourselves. Ordinary events tend to take on the gravity of life or death matters, and we can end up with high blood pressure or some other equally miserable consequence of what is actually self-induced stress.

Mentally healthy people maintain a healthy perspective on what's happening in their lives. They participate in life almost as if they were characters in a play, giving themselves to each and every scene but never losing their perspective. Even when a scene appears to be very dramatic, it's as if they say to themselves, "Play your part, but remember that it's just a play, and you need not take the drama of it too seriously." In the authors' view, this is the intended meaning of the biblical admonishment to "be in the world, but not of it."

They also have an understanding of life that recalls Shakespeare, who wrote, "The play's the thing."* That is,

---

*William Shakespeare, *Hamlet*, act 2, sc. 2, line 604.

mentally healthy people realize that the more they are present to give themselves to the reality of each moment, the more fun it is to participate in life, and the more fulfilling life is as well. This play-full attitude permeates their every interaction with the world.

In the actual play of life, sincerity is the mark of mental health and insincerity is the equivalent of lousy acting. To act phony or like a hypocrite is not only unhealthy, but is also likely to ruin the scene for everyone involved.

We can choose to play our parts in life as if we were in a grade-B movie or in a potential Academy Award winner. By being sincere and expressing ourselves truthfully, we can touch the hearts of others by showing the world a truly genuine human being. This quality of authenticity is what makes for a lively, award-winning life.

Red Barber, the famous sportscaster, said that when we imitate someone else, we dilute our own wine. Mentally healthy people have discovered a way to maintain the full-bodied flavor of themselves, so their every interaction becomes a toast to life itself.

INSIGHT 37
FREE OF BELIEFS

(I) n this book, the word "beliefs" is used to refer to thoughts that exist strictly on a mental, intellectual, and philosophical plane. Our beliefs have to do with what we imagine is true or not true. In contrast, there is the verb "to know" in its various forms, used to represent a deeper, more organic aspect of the Self. We *know* something to be true or not true only through direct experience of it. For example, it is one thing to look at a picture of a bowl of pasta and believe (imagine) it would taste delicious; it's quite another thing to actually eat a bowl of pasta and *know* how delicious it tastes.

In Saint-Exupery's superb book, *The Little Prince*, the fox says to the prince, "It is only with the heart that one can see clearly. What is essential is 'invisible' to the eyes."* One interpretation of this lovely passage is that beliefs exist only in our heads—in the linear thinking mind—whereas knowing exists in our hearts—in the reality of experience. Ultimately, we know something to be true because we feel it to be so, not because we think or believe it is so.

In the realm of knowing there are three distinct possibilities: (1) we know something is true, (2) we know it is

---

*Antoine de Saint-Exupery, *The Little Prince* (New York: Harcourt, Brace, 1945).

false, or (3) we don't yet know whether it's true or false. Beliefs are needed only in the last instance when in reality, we are unsure of something. In essence, when we believe or disbelieve something we are trying to convince ourselves, one way or the other, of something we don't really know.

Mentally healthy people live on the basis of what they know—not what they believe. Take the question of flying saucers, for example. Assuming there's been no direct experience with them, mentally healthy people neither believe nor disbelieve in the existence of UFOs. They simply don't know whether such phenomena exist or not. Uncertainty is not a problem for them. In fact, they find that living with uncertainty turns life into a great adventure.

In the last years of his life, the great Swiss psychiatrist, Dr. Carl Jung, was interviewed on TV by the British Broadcasting Company. When asked if he believed in God, Jung smiled and, in essence, said that he didn't. His answer took the British interviewer aback, and he asked Dr. Jung how that could be in light of his writings on the matter. Jung responded quite tenderly that he "knew" God and therefore had no need to believe in God.

INSIGHT 38
FREE OF OPINIONS

There is an important distinction between opinions—mental judgments, and feelings—visceral awarenesses. Sometimes opinions can be accompanied by feelings, even very strong feelings; but in essence, they exist in different realms altogether. Opinions exist in the realm of the intellect or thinking mind—the realm of imagining.

According to Webster's dictionary, opinions are "less strong than positive knowledge." That is to say they exist as ideas which are thought or believed to be true but not actually *known* to be true. Very often opinions have moralistic overtones because they address matters of right and wrong. It is interesting to note the demeanor of most opinionated people. They tend to be rather defensive in their interpersonal dealings. Often they want to argue their point of view to prove they are right in what they believe. They also tend to be closed-minded people who give the impression of being rather self-righteous.

People who are mentally healthy, on the other hand, are very open-minded, with a great capacity and willingness to see things from differing points of view. Although they don't hesitate to express themselves, they do not engage in arguing. They understand that opposite points of view need not be in opposition. For the most part, their focus is on how they feel about things, and that is what

87

they choose to talk about. They are generally not interested in making moral judgments and thus have very little to say when it comes to such things.

There's an old joke that opinions are like a certain body part—everyone's got one and they all smell! Perhaps that's a little on the strong side, but as a general rule, the healthier we are the less emphasis we place on opinions—ours or anyone else's.

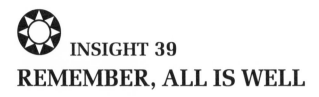

INSIGHT 39
REMEMBER, ALL IS WELL

I t's easy to have faith when things are going the way we want them to go. Then we feel that all is well with the world. Maintaining that perspective when circumstances are unpleasant, however, is another thing entirely. So often it seems that in the face of difficult circumstances, people resort to negative thinking. They start complaining that this is wrong or that is wrong, and before you know it, they move into the harsh realm of condemnation.

Mentally healthy people embody a kind of faith that is not limited to times when things are going the way they want them to go. It is a faith that knows no bounds, allowing them to appreciate times of sorrow as well as times of joy, times of disturbance as well as times of calm. This is the kind of faith that Albert Camus must have had when he wrote that in the depths of winter he discovered an invincible summer living within him. Such a faith is related to a deep and abiding awareness that, regardless of appearances, things are always fitting together somehow—even though we may not understand the particulars of how or why. It is a faith that is unlimited, always embracing things just the way they are.

Mentally healthy people know in their hearts the truthfulness of the saying, "Things always happen for the best," and their living expresses that knowing. It is this sense of the fittingness of all things that is central to their world view. In a very real way, this understanding is the essence of what wisdom truly is.

There is a wonderful story about a great spiritual leader who was walking along a narrow mountain path at the edge of a cliff. There were multicolored flowers all along the path. His followers were walking in single file behind him. Suddenly, his foot slipped and he lost his balance. As he was about to fall to his certain death, his disciples heard him say from below, "What a beautiful flower!"

Imagine having a faith so strong that even impending pain and death is not cause for fear or distress. That would truly take care of all our worries, wouldn't it?

 **INSIGHT 40**
FREE TO BE

any of our fears seem to be related to the idea of failure. It has become a common way of dealing with life to evaluate everything we do in terms of how it measures up to some preordained, arbitrary standard. We often compare our level of achievement to the performance of others. The effect of this cultural obsession with "success versus failure" is a lack of spontaneity in our self-expression and a lack of creativity as well.

Mentally healthy people have escaped from the bondage of the obsessive concern about success and failure. Thus, they have no need to engage in mental deliberation; that is, to spend time figuring out what to do in a given situation. Rather, their actions emerge simultaneously with the situation that calls for them. In nature, animals respond appropriately to their surroundings without prior thought, and so do mentally healthy people as they exhibit a deep trust in their nature and their capacity to respond spontaneously and appropriately to what is happening. Whatever their response—which sometimes is no response at all—it is felt to be the naturally fitting piece to the puzzle of life at that moment. They do not spend time deliberating or worrying over what to do, and they don't second guess themselves, either. Second guessing ("If only I'd done this instead of that . . .") is a great way for people to drive themselves crazy. It's called 20/20 hindsight.

Deliberation is an interesting word. The prefix "de" means the opposite of, and liberation means freedom. So the word literally means "the opposite of freedom." And what is the opposite of freedom? Obviously, it's slavery; and people who have a habit of always deliberating before they respond are enslaved by the thinking mind.

Mental health is really about freedom—the freedom to be naturally and spontaneously ourselves. Shakespeare's Hamlet revealed a deep understanding of this when he said, "To be or not to be, that is the question."* That is the question, indeed.

---

*William Shakespeare, *Hamlet,* act 3, sc. 1, line 56.

 INSIGHT 41

LIVE IN DELIGHTFUL UNCERTAINTY

For many people, life has lost its edge. Day to day activities often feel like drudgery, and there is a constant struggle to overcome an underlying sense of stagnation and boredom. Such a state of mind comes from a gross misunderstanding of reality. It comes from the belief that we know what life is supposed to be about—getting things, having things, accomplishing things, etc.—and that all there is to do is try to manipulate circumstances to achieve our goals, wherever and whenever possible. The problem with this way of thinking is that even when we do manage to achieve a goal, it doesn't provide any lasting sense of fulfillment. As a matter of fact, it is common to end up feeling a sense of letdown and disappointment after a goal has been achieved.

Another consequence of this misunderstanding of reality is the perception that every day is essentially a repeat of the day before. Rarely is anything experienced as fresh and new, and life takes on the tragicomic image of a dog chasing after its own tail.

Mentally healthy people have a different point of view. They realize that they don't really know what life is supposed to be. Thus their minds are open, and they are essentially free of preconceived ideas and beliefs about what any given situation is all about. When they enter a situation, who ultimately might be affected by that situa-

93

tion and how they might be affected, is uncertain as far as they know. They do not attempt to make premeditated, calculated responses based on imagined assumptions about what is about to occur. They simply rely on their capacity to respond spontaneously and intuitively to the contingencies of each moment as these contingencies present themselves. In this way, mentally healthy people are open to all the creative possibilities that exist as life unfolds.

There's an old song that begins, "Ah sweet mystery of life," and those words echo the sentiment of mentally healthy people. They live with a divine sense of uncertainty, and as a result, life is a truly wonderful adventure. They experience a freshness and vitality in living each new day. As you can imagine, they rarely, if ever, get bored. Like the experience of reading a good mystery novel, living with delightful uncertainty has a way of generating an ongoing interest in life—and even an occasional dose of real excitement.

Mentally healthy people view every present moment as bringing sort of a surprise "present" to them. They are constantly enlivened by whatever happens. This way of being makes life a lot more fun than it would be if we were able to know what our "presents" were going to be before they even arrived.

Conclusion

Artful living is about awareness. It's about being present to consciously experience the ever-changing "now" moment by moment. In a way, it's like being married to reality; for it's a commitment to participate in life fully, for richer or poorer, in joy and in sorrow, in sickness and in health. No experience is rejected from consciousness or denied in the body, and nothing is more important or precious than the bottom line awareness of being alive. This quality of aliveness, is always available to be realized, and has enormous intrinsic value. There is no need to desperately seek value outside our own being.

Artful living is about relaxation—true and deep relaxation. Like water being drawn into a sponge, we find ourselves effortlessly absorbed into the shifting currents of life. Resting comfortably at home with ourselves, it seems there is no way to resist life. Nor is there any need to do so. We are relaxed because we are content just to be, and we know that the gift of life is really the gift of being present to consciously experience life. It is by accepting this gift that we are able to offer our own unique gifts to the world.

Artful living is about JOY. Whatever consciously aware people do is done joyfully, because real joy comes from the simple appreciation of being alive. From this perspective, the specifics of what we do at any given moment don't matter all that much. This joy stems from an unmistakable sense of wholeness within that transcends any need for a relationship, or a good job, or anything else. We are fully ourselves and that seems to be plenty. Living takes on a joy-full quality which brings to mind the refrain of another old song, "I've got plenty of nothing, and nothing's plenty for me."

Artful living is about serenity. It's like residing in the depths of the ocean where, regardless of what is happening on the surface, there is an incredible stillness and calm. Serenity is a feeling so deep and profound that experiences of pleasure and pain come and go like waves on the surface of existence. They don't really have much of an effect because at the ocean depths, surface phenomena are only felt as ripples. Mental health involves a commitment to life as a process of growth—a process involving a series of deaths and rebirths whereby our sense of separateness and selfishness is replaced with a growing sense of oneness and a feeling of love for all living things.

An ancient teaching suggests that there are four basic groups of people in the world; those who don't know, but don't know that they don't know; those who also don't know, but know that they don't know; those who do know, but don't know that they know; and finally, those who know, and know that they know.

The first group, which is probably the largest, are people who don't know the state of mental health but don't know that they don't know. They are really in the dark—mistaking their opinions and beliefs for the truth and their dreams for reality. It is highly unlikely such people would be interested in reading a book like this. For one thing, they're probably too busy watching television.

The second group, according to lore, is composed of people who also don't know the state of mental health but know that they don't know. Such people are ready to begin the process of self-inquiry that will lead them beyond mere mental understanding to the promised land of Loving Being. People in this group are like ripe pieces of fruit—ready to drop from the parent tree and allow nature's creative process to transform their existence into a whole new reality.

The third group includes people who do know the state of mental health, but don't know that they know.

This group probably contains the fewest people. They are the ones who have a deep feeling of serenity—though they're so absorbed in it, they wouldn't even be able to say they were serene. In some Native American traditions, such people are called "mudheads," and they are held in very high esteem by the rest of the community.

Finally, there is the fourth group—those who know the state of mental health, and know that they know. According to the lore, these are the true teachers of mental health. In the Native American tradition, they are called shamans. In the East, they are known as enlightened masters. They are easily recognizable by their tendency to comfort the afflicted and afflict the comfortable. Of course, the thing they know above all else is that mental health cannot be taught. That is what makes them such great teachers.

Now go back over the insights and determine which of these four groups you belong in. To do this, you need to count the number of insights that you actually embody in daily life. If your score is zero, you're definitely in the first group—and probably will never want to read a book like this again. If you score is between one and 10, you're in the second group—definitely a little fruity and ripe for stewing. If your score is between 11 and 40, congratulations, you're a mudhead. And if you embody all 41 insights, please call us as soon as possible—we need your help!

97

Index

A

ability to confide, 34
adaptability, 13
addictions, 51
alcohol, 51
alien, 51
alienation, 45
all is well, 89
all the world's a stage, 24
Allen Woody, 6
angels fly, 16
anti-blame program, 56
appreciation, 21
arguments, 59
arrogance, 61
avoiding pain, 13
awareness, 67

B

be here now, 73
be sincere, not serious, 93
befriend each moment, 7
being, 19, 32
being is loving, 43
being superior, 23
bird, 29
birds of sadness, 53
blame, 55
Blake, William, 65
block out, 31

boredom, 93
breathing, 39
Bradley, Man'on Zimmer, 36, 38
bribes, 59
by-passing our hearts, 58

C

Campbell, Joseph, 32
Camus, Albert, 89
cat, 29
child like, 67
Chinese sage, 34
choices, 13
chronic shallow breathing, 40
circumstances, 13
clinical depression, 45
closed-minded, 87
co-dependency, 46
coercion, 59
coma, 45
comfort, 13
commitment, 13, 96
communicate feelings honestly, 49
communication, 49
comparing, 47
compassion, 29
complaining, 7

cowardice, 80
creative nature of feelings, 77
criticizing, 7
cultivate self-love, 21

D

denial, 31
desires, 15
direct experience, 5
disappointment, 93
discomfort, 13
don't ask why, 5
drugs, 51
dysfunctional family, 5

E

Einstein, Albert, 6, 78
emotion, 31, 77
emotional grounding, 37
emotional investment, 3
empowerment, 46
enjoy being ordinary, 23
enlightened masters, 97
enslaved by thoughts, 47
Exodus, 51
expectation, 3, 4
experience, 77

F

faith, 89
fault-finding, 55

fears, 91
feeling/emotional nature, 50, 75
feelings, 33, 49, 75, 77
finger-pointing, 7, 55
flexibility, 13
flow and change, 53
free of arrogance, 61
free of beliefs, 85
free of quilt, 35
free of judging, 69
free of opinions, 87
free to be, 91
frustration, 65, 81
fundamental relationship, 44

G

Gallagher, Jim, 22
gambling, 51
going with flow, 3
goodness, 21
greed, 51
guilt, 35, 59

H

happily ever after, 37
harmony, 15
helplessness, 81
Henry, 9
honesty, 17
honor the body, 25

horse, 70
hostility, 57
humility, 23, 79
Humpty Dumpty, 24

I

ignorance, 79, 80
image of outer world, 77
impotence, 82
insecurity, 61, 76
insights, 97
integrity, 13, 17
internal well-being, 51
intimacy, 45, 46
intimacy with life, 45
IQ, 61
isolation, 45

J

joy, 95
judging, 69
Jung, C.G., 86

L

laughter, 34
life is a mystery, 65
listening, 73
live and let live, 59
live in harmony with
    desires, 15
live life as a struggle, 7

living with delightful
    uncertainty, 93
loving, 43

M

Malden, Karl, 4
Merlin, 36
misfortune, 70
more is better, 19
Muggerudge, Malcolm, 7

N

negative beliefs, 21
no good deed goes unpub-
    lished, 62
no need to get even, 57
not knowing, 80

O

obsessive concern about
    success, 91
opinions, 87
ordinary, 23
oughts, 17
owning experience, 77

P

pain, 53
pain, avoiding, 13
perception in perspective,
    19

personal empowerment, 78
personal preferences secondary, 13
perspective, 19
play-full attitude, 84
play's the thing, 83
Popeye the Sailorman, 52
power, 51
present moment, 73

R

rationalizing circumstances, 65
reality, 93
re-evaluate values, 17
relationship, 44, 49, 59, 95
relaxation, 95
resentment, 81
respect, 21
responsible behavior, 81
roots, 76
row your boat, 8

S

Saint-Exupery, Antoine de, 85
sarcasm, 57
satisfaction, 19
say no to blame, 55
seeking pleasure, 13
self, 85
self-actualization, 20

self-appreciation, 21, 52
self-awareness, 75
self-deception, 32
self-doubt, 76
self-esteem, 15, 21, 54
self-importance, 23
self-love, 21
self-pity, 82
self-respect, 21, 25
self-righteous, 87
self-sacrifice, 82
self-satisfaction, 15, 19
sense of wonder, 67
sex, 51
Shakespeare, William, 18, 24, 83, 92
shaman, 97
shame-based reality, 33
sharing and comparing, 47
shoulds, 17, 69
show true feelings, 33
sound body, sound mind, 25
soul, 19
sparrow, 9
stagnation, 93
stress, 59
stress-free living, 39
suffering, 53, 59

T

taking responsibility, 49
thinking mind, 47
Thoreau, H. D., 19

Tolstoy, Leo, 74
total acceptance, 9
trials and tribulations, 23
trust real feelings, 75
20/20 hindsight, 91

U

uncertainty, 93
unhappiness, ongoing, 5
Ustinov, Peter, 80

V

value every emotion, 31
value not knowing, 79
values, 17
victim mentality, 54, 81

victims no more, 53
Vonnegut, Kurt, 5

W

want what happens, 9
whining, 7
why, 5
Wilde, Oscar, 15
Winkler, Henry, 22
wisdom of the universe, 79
wood cutter, 69

Y

yummies, 66
yuppies, 66

Isaac David Shamaya earned his Ph.D. in clinical psychology from the University of Massachusetts in 1970. Following a major life transformation, he left his private psychotherapy practice in 1981 to study meditation and pursue his own spiritual journey. He has worked in the field of addiction treatment and now lectures and conducts seminars on emotional healing and spiritual living. He is the author of several other books including *So Speaks Higher Power* and *What I Wish for You*. He currently lives with his wife Alexandra in Tuscon, AZ.

Ron Fortier

Carolyn Shamaya received a Bachelor's degree in fine arts and biology in 1962 from George Peabody College of Vanderbilt University in Nashville, TN. She later returned for a Master's degree in education. She has served as a hospital administrator in three different residential facilities, and as a program director in a variety of community based projects for developmentally disabled persons. She has also worked as a psychotherapist and is presently employed in the administrative offices of New Mexico's Division of Mental Health. Carolyn's first book, published in 1990 and co-authored with Louis Wynne, Ph.D., is titled *Warm Logic: The Art of the Intuitive Lifestyle* (Skidmore-Roth). She is currently completing a series of meditation tapes based on spiritual messages gathered over the past four years. Carolyn resides in Santa Fe, NM.